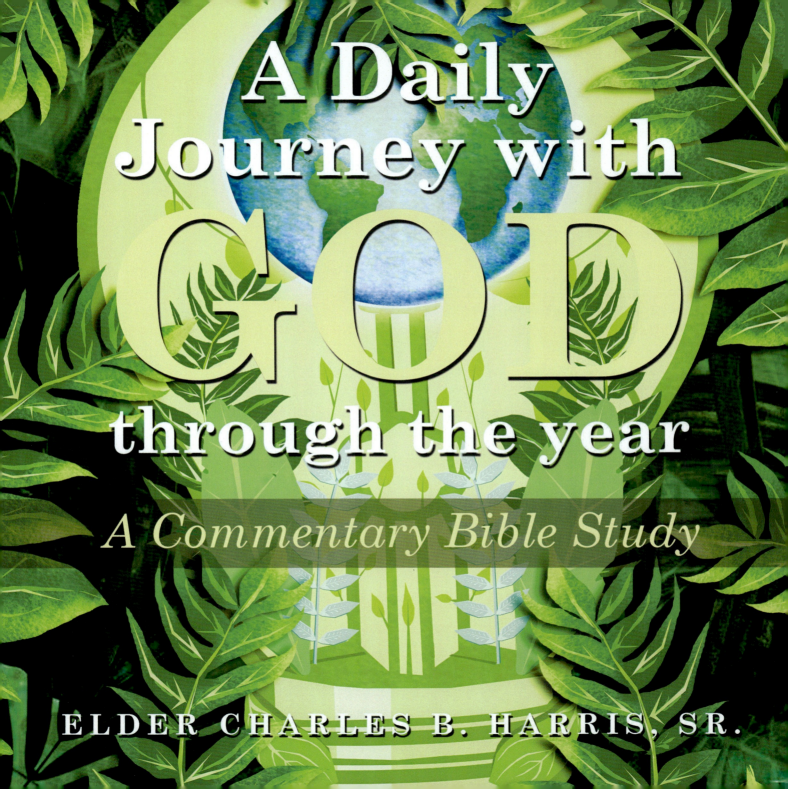

To order additional copies of this book, contact:
Xlibris
844-714-8691
www.Xlibris.com
Orders@Xlibris.com

KJV
Scripture quotations marked KJV are from the Holy Bible, King James Version (Authorized Version). First published in 1611. Quoted from the KJV Classic Reference Bible, Copyright © 1983 by The Zondervan Corporation.

NIV
Scripture quotations marked NIV are taken from the Holy Bible, New International Version®. NIV®. Copyright © 1973, 1978, 1984 by International Bible Society. Used by permission of Zondervan. All rights reserved. [Biblica]

ESV
Unless otherwise indicated, all scripture quotations are from The Holy Bible, English Standard Version® (ESV®). Copyright ©2001 by Crossway Bibles, a division of Good News Publishers. Used by permission. All rights reserved.

NKJV
Scripture quotations marked NKJV are taken from the New King James Version. Copyright © 1982 by Thomas Nelson, Inc. Used by permission. All rights reserved.

ISBN:     Softcover        978-1-6641-7914-1
          Hardcover        978-1-6641-7915-8
          EBook            978-1-6641-7916-5

Print information available on the last page

Rev. date: 06/15/2021

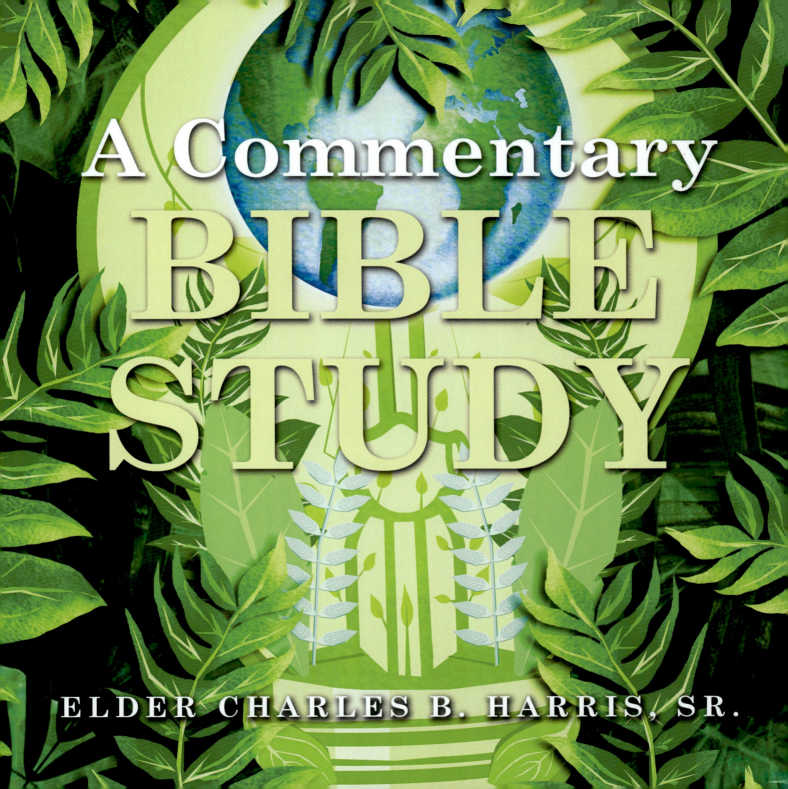

# A Commentary
# BIBLE
# STUDY

ELDER CHARLES B. HARRIS, SR.

# Dedication

IN LOVING MEMORY OF OUR BELOVED PARENTS

HON. MELVILLE F. HARRIS SR.

JOSEPHINE B. HARRIS

MARY AMMONS (Mother in Law)

And
OUR BELOVED SISTER
REV. HANNAH HARRIS PETERSON

**A SPECIAL GIFT**
**A Daily Journey**
**With God Through the Year,**
**A Commentary Bible Study**
**Presented**:

**TO**: _____

**DATE**: _____

**FROM**:_____

# Contents

# From The Author's Desk

ACCORDING TO THE notes collected from my desk, there are many spiritual benefits one will receive while he or she is undertaking *A Daily Journey with God Through The Year*, and a few examples of those blessings are as follows: peace, love, joy, happiness, protection against all evil spirits, longevity, etc.

Believers of Christ, if you will be obedient to the Word of the Lord by undertaking "A Spiritual Journey with God," beginning this New Year, January 1ˢᵗ, while you are looking up to the cross of Calvary and putting your whole trust in God, you and your family will surely be blessed.

I have a living testimony to share with you, Christian friends, what the Lord has done for me, but I cannot tell it all because of the limitation of time. Many years ago, I was caught up between life and death on two different occasions, but I prayed sincerely with FAITH to the Lord, and God Almighty arrived just in time. He blessed me by saving my life from the enemies. I, therefore, made some bold claims about this "Commentary Bible Study" based on my FAITH and trust in God. I will encourage you, brethren, to exercise your FAITH as you study and act on the Word of God in order for you to make your own claim about this Commentary Bible Study, realizing that FAITH without works is dead (James 2:17–18). But, in my distress, I cried unto the Lord, and He heard me (Psalm 120:1–7 kjv).

If it had not been for the Lord, who was on my side, when men rose up against me, they would have swallowed me up quickly when their wrath was kindled against me (Psalm 124:1–8).

Therefore, I am very grateful to the Lord for saving my life from the hands of those ungodly people, and I will continue to serve Him as I praise His holy name, for His goodness and mercy endureth forever, because His name is worthy to be praised. Believers of Christ, just keep in mind that anything you ask of the Lord, with FAITH, you shall receive, because FAITH is the substance of things hoped for, and the evidence of things not seen (Matthew 7:7–8; Hebrews 11:1–2 kjv).

Exactly two years ago, I decided to undertake "A Daily Journey With God," along with my beloved wife Victoria, as well as other family members and friends. From the day we started studying the Bible together, from Genesis to Revelation, my whole life has changed for good. As a result, I have never been the same person anymore, because all of the things I used to do before our Bible group study I do them no more. Praise the Lord!

Let me tell you a story, Christian friends, about a faithful servant of God who studied the Word of God consistently, every day, and who recently testified that his doctor had given him up to die because of his illness. Unfortunately, his wife and family members were making an arrangement to put him in a House Peace Center. This servant of God who always believed in the healing power of the Lord prayed to God Almighty, with FAITH, and he was healed instantly by the God of Abraham, Isaac, and Jacob. This surely was the power of God. Amen!

Therefore, remember that "In consistency lies the power," and because of your FAITH in God, your prayer WILL be answered whenever you wait patiently upon the Lord, whether in good or bad times, of your life.

## A DAILY JOURNEY WITH GOD, THROUGH THE YEAR

Believers in Christ, there is nothing impossible for the Lord to do for you. Just humble yourself in the sight of the Lord, and He will lift you up because He is a God that never fails. You just need to be focused and look up to "The Hill," just as David did, from whence cometh your help (James 4:10–11 kjv; Psalm 121:1–2 kjv).

I have decided to work for the Lord, and there is no turning back for me whatsoever. That is why I have written this *Commentary Bible Study: A Journey With God* in order that you, your family, and friends can also be blessed. All you have to do is to pick up the cross and follow Jesus in undertaking *A Daily Journey With God Through The Year.* By so doing, this will definitely give hope to others in witnessing for Christ as well as saving lives, and at the same time, winning souls to Christ.

The Bible teaches us that before Christ came on earth to die for our sins, there were man y faithful servants of God who were blessed because they served the Lord, and a few of those servants are as follow: Adam, Seth, Jared, Enoch, Methuselah, Abraham, Isaac, Jacob, Joseph, Moses, Aaron, Joshua, Naomi, Ruth, Hannah, Esther, Eli, Samuel, David, Solomon, Nathan, Elijah, Elisha, Hezekiah, Benjamin, Joe, Isaiah, Jeremiah, Ezekiel, Daniel, Shadrach, Meshach, Abednego, Jonah, Zechariah, Dr. Martin L. King Jr., etc.

Christian brothers, and sisters, while you are on your 365-day journey with the Lord, please be reminded that you will definitely be tempted by the devil. Nevertheless, you need to be strong with your FAITH, and also, you need to be grounded in the Lord. "By resisting the devil, he shall flee from you" (James 4:7–8 niv). This Commentary Bible Study will be used as a quick reference guide whenever Christians are faced with their daily earthly challenges. Therefore, renew your FAITH in the Lord, because He loves, and He cares for all of His children, regardless of religion, nationality, race, or color.

As you walk your daily journey with the Lord, you will observe that the Powerhouse of God will be opened unto you 24/7 to receive, and to answer, all of your prayers, with FAITH, regardless of whether you are asking the good Lord for the forgiveness of your sins, or you are seeking His holy blessing regarding your illness, a job, traveling mercies, protection against evil forces, your daily and school activities, accidents, etc. Also, if you are asking God for a husband, a wife, or a child, a house, a car, or even a business opportunity, just take this *Daily Journey With God* mixed with a little FAITH for a positive result of your prayers. There is a "Spiritual Heavenly Hotline" which is free of charge, and it was installed from earth to heaven thousands of years ago by Jesus Christ, I strongly believe. This "hotline" is available 24/7 to all believers of Christ, but you need to demonstrate FAITH whenever you dial the "hotline" 911-JESUS, and your prayers will be answered immediately. Remember, you do not need an animal sacrifice offering before dialing the "hotline." Just dial directly for yourself, because Christ is risen from the dead, and He is alive. Remember, Jesus paid the price for your sins with His blood, so that we, through Him, can live.

Believers of Christ, as you study this Commentary Bible, you will become closer to God; you will abide in Him, and He in you. Also, your FAITH will be strengthened in the Lord, and you will gain more wisdom, knowledge, and understanding as you study the Bible. Brethren, while you are walking every day with the Lord on your journey, you will learn how to call upon Jesus whenever you need Him, whether in good or bad times of your life. Also, you will study about the "Springboard and Instruments" of David, as well as the "Temptation of Jesus," from the beginning of His journey, and His last journey on earth, before His death.

Christian friends, if you are willing and obedient, ye shall eat the good of the land. But if you refuse and rebel, ye shall be devoured with the sword, for the mouth of the Lord hath spoken it (Isaiah 1:19–20 kjv). As you fast and pray with FAITH while you are on your *Daily Journey With God*, please focus on the overview of the Old and the New Testaments. The Old Testament predicts the coming of the MESSIAH, whereas, the New Testament is the fulfillment of God's promises to His people regarding the birth of JESUS CHRIST. AMEN! Therefore, believers of Christ, the ball is in your court to do the right thing by undertaking *A Daily Journey With God* this coming New Year's Eve, not just for a relative or a friend, but for yourself, because God will open His window of many blessings upon you and your family if only you will trust and obey.

Finally, and foremost, Christian brothers and sisters, we are presently living in the last days of our lives, and we do not know the day or the hour of the coming of the Lord. Therefore, you must always encourage somebody to undertake their own daily journey with God as we prepare ourselves for our "final journey" with the Lord, when the saints of God are marching with Jesus Christ to heaven. Do you want to be in that number, Christian friends, when the roll is called in heaven? "Praise God from whom all blessings flow, let everything that hath breath, praise the Lord. Praise ye the Lord" (Psalm 150:1–6 kjv). Amen! Your humble servant of the Lord, **Elder: Charles B. Harris Sr.**

# Acknowledgment

**MY SINCERE THANKS and appreciation to all those many relatives and friends who encouraged me to write *A Daily Journey With God Through The Year*.**

Special gratitude goes to my beloved wife, Rev. Victoria Gooding Harris, who prayed, encouraged, and stood by my side every step of the way as I wrote this Commentary Bible Study.

Thanks, also, to my brothers and sisters and to my children for their love and support, including my nephew, Prophet Wilta T. Harris.

I am very grateful to Rev. Sylvia Simpson, Mr. Ernest Cassell, Rev. Dr. William B. G. K. Harris, Rev. Dr. Abayomi Noibi, Elder Siahyonkron Nyanseor, Rev. Dr. Peter Z. M. Nehsahn, Rev. Sam Eddie Gibson, Rev Theophilus Massaquoi, Rev. Emanuel Henighan, Rev. Jukontee Kebbeh, Brother Karlton Davis, and others, for their technical support toward this project.

**Finally, I praise God from whom all blessings flow, and I am very grateful for all the wonderful things the good Lord has done in my life, including giving me the patience, knowledge, and the wisdom to me to write *A Daily Journey with God Through the Year*.** Amen!

xvi

# 1 Foreword

THIS IS AN imperfect book. It is imperfect in its language, structure, and narrative. Nevertheless, this book, *A Journey with God Through the Year*, is made perfect by the grace of God from His throne.

This book is of special concern to the author, Elder Charles B. Harris, a retired civil engineer, because of his own personal journey with the Word of God. Elder Harris's own personal journey led him to write this book, trusting the Word of God in Psalm 138:8 in the New King James Version that said that "The Lord will perfect that which concerns me" by His grace.

There is no better way of knowing Him than to study His WORD. The Lord will perfect everything about you as you put your daily study of His into action. Guided by the Spirit in your study, you will be able to testify with Job, "I know that my redeemer liveth, and that he shall stand at the latter day upon the earth" (Job 19:25 kjv).

May God bless and perfect those who use this book, *A Daily Journey With God Through The Year*. Trust the WORD and eagerly wait for the manifestations of the power of God in your lives.

**The Spirit of the Living God Speaks!!!**

# 2 Introduction

THERE ARE SEVERAL **"events"** which occurred in each chapter of the Old and New Testaments for the very first time, and we, as believers of Christ, need to study and understand those **"event**s" as we share God's message around the world. Therefore, Christian brothers and sisters, by undertaking *A Daily Journey With God Through The Year,* it will definitely strengthen our **FAITH** in the Lord, as well as enhance our personal relationship with God.

For a very long time, believers of Christ have been teaching and spreading the Gospel of Jesus Christ all around the world. Nevertheless, that grand old dragon called the devil, or Satan, has tried, unsuccessfully, over the past years, to stop God's words from spreading. As you take **"A GLANCE AT A FEW EVENTS OF The BIBLE"** while on **"Your Daily Journey With The Lord,"** you must tell the devil that he is a liar, and you will always serve the true and the living God of Abraham, Isaac, and Jacob.

## TEMPTATION

Recall that when Christ told the devil for the very first time when He was tempted during His forty days and forty nights of fasting in the wilderness . . . Then Jesus said unto Satan: "Get thee hence, Satan; for it is written, thou shall worship the Lord thy God, and only Him shall thou serve."

Therefore, Christian friends, while you are on your *Daily Journey With God Through The Year*, you must always remember to tell the devil to "Get thee hence," in times of temptation whenever you are carrying out God's work**.**

## CALL UPON THE LORD

Believers of Christ, whenever you are undertaking your **Daily Journey With God,** whether it is in bad times or in good times of your life, or during your trials and tribulations, as you take **a glance at the Bible,** you must always **call upon the Lord (the Alpha and the Omega).** Jesus has paid the price for our sins with His blood when He was crucified on the **Cross of Calvary** (Luke 23:34; John 19:20; Matthew 27:46 NIV). Generally, most believers of Christ only **call upon the LORD** whenever they have sinned, or during times of illness, long suffering, and whenever they need hope and guidance, especially when a person has disappointed them. Also, they usually call upon God for help whenever they are tempted by the devil. However, God directed His people to *always* **call upon Him,** whether in the midst of a crisis or during normal situations (Psalm 18:3–36; Psalm 34:5–6 NIV). In comparing believers in Christ to the nonbelievers, I strongly believe that nonbelievers will only **CALL UPON GOD** in times of an emergency or whenever they are in trouble. They have no **FAITH** in God. In my opinion, the nonbelievers will always be thinking that there is a god somewhere, a strange god who is forever waiting and ready to rescue them from trouble. They are wrong because their strange god has no power. I believe that if a nonbeliever needs the true and the living God's protection in times of emergencies, or in times of trouble, he or she must first pick up the **"cross,"** and follow the Lord. The Lord is faithful and just to forgive us from our sins and to cleanse us from all unrighteousness, if only we confess our sins to Him. A believer in Christ has a strong faith in God, whereas, the nonbelievers have no faith in God. This is the difference between a believer and a nonbeliever (1 John 1:9–10; Romans 3:26–27).

## SPRINGBOARD AND INSTRUMENT

This **Daily Journey With God Through The Year** is not meant to alter or to replace the Holy Bible; but rather, it must be used as a spiritual springboard and instrument in saving lives and winning souls for Christ. It must also be used as a commentary Bible. Recall that King David was leaping in the air and dancing with all his might while he was carrying the Ark of God into the city of David with the best musical instruments of Israel. King David was bouncing up and down just like a springboard for the Lord. David's wife, the daughter of Saul, despised her husband, the king, because he danced publicly in the midst of all Israel for the Lord by uncovering himself for the very first time, I believe, in the eyes of his handmaids and servants. However, King David replied to his wife, Michal, by saying unto her: "I will play before the Lord, my God." After this, Michal had no child unto the day of her death (2 Samuel 6:20–23 kjv).

**A Glance At The Bible** informs us that King David instructed all believers to always: "Praise ye the Lord with all types of musical instruments, and dance, including everything that hath breath and must praise the Lord" (Psalm 150:1–6 kjv). Therefore, Christian brothers and sisters, this ***Daily Journey With God*** must serve as a **quick reference guide** whenever we, as believers of Christ, are faced with the daily earthly challenges by witnessing for Christ and swearing about His existence and His power, and also defending God's Word. God has promised us that His kingdom will come, and His will be done on earth as it is in heaven, because He gave unto us His only begotten Son (John 3:16–18 kjv).

My dear brethren, **A GLANCE AT THE BIBLE** must, and should always be, read and studied with faithfulness, prayers, and conviction because whatsoever God says in His Word will surely come to pass (Ezekiel 12:25–26). Therefore, as you undertake your ***Daily Journey With God Through The Year,*** it will definitely bring you closer to God. This journey will also give you wisdom, understanding, peace of mind, as well as patience and love as you deal with your fellow men. Amen!

## THE POWERHOUSE OF GOD

**The Powerhouse of God is where we as believers of Christ received our entire blessings directly from the Lord.** This heavenly spiritual house is open 24/7 for all of God's children as we seek His blessings and put all of our trust in Him as our Lord and Master. Whenever you are undertaking your ***Daily Journey With God Through The Year,*** **you must definitely believe and have faith in the Lord that this powerhouse of God** brings peace, love, joy, and happiness. It also strengthens your **faith** in the **Lord,** as well as enhances your personal relationship with **God.**

Christian brothers and sisters, as you undertake your ***Daily Journey With God Through The Year,*** **you must always remember that you are a child of God, and Jesus loves you.** Recall that Jesus shed His blood for our sins on that **old rugged Cross of Calvary,** so that we too can live. In my opinion, Jesus installed **"a spiritual heavenly emergency hotline"** directly from earth to heaven thousands of years ago, and that emergency number is known as: **"911-JESUS."** This spiritual hotline is **free of charge, and Jesus is waiting for your calls 24/7, at the receiving end of the line in order to answer your prayers and also solve all of your problems . . . if only**

**you believe and have faith in Him**. Christian friends, remember that "**faith** is the substance of things hoped for, and the evidence of things not seen" (Hebrews 11:1–2 kjv). All things are possible with **God**, and with just a little **faith,** anything you ask of the **Lord**, you shall receive (Matthew 7:7–8).

Finally, brethren, one must always **look up to God** during your ***Daily Journey With The Lord*** in order to receive an answer to your prayer from the **Lord,** including a blessing directly from "**from the powerhouse of God."** Praise the **Lord!**

## A GLANCE AT A FEW EVENTS OF THE BIBLE

Believers of Christ, just **take a glance** at a few of the very first events of the Old and the New Testaments as you continue Your ***Daily Journey With God Through The Year.* In my opinion, this will enable you to study and to quickly answer all of those questions that are listed below in the Bible, as follows:**

**The Old Testament**

(1) What were the first two great lights of God's creation?

(2) The first great creature of the sea that was created by God, before Adam and Eve, was called what?

(3) The first medical doctor and his successful major surgical operation. Who was he?

(4) The first marriage (wedding). Where did it take place, and who administered the wedding?

(5) The first gardener on earth was called Joseph. True or false?

(6) The first temptation after God's creation was done by Abraham. True or false?

(7) The first punishment on earth. Name the punishment that was given, and to whom was this punishment given?

(8) The first child to be born on earth. What was his name?

(9) The first killer on the face of the earth was called King Saul. True or false?

(10) The first fugitive ever known was called Jacob. True or false?

(11) One of the very first farmers on earth. What was his name?

(12) One of the first shepherd boys was called David. True or false?

(13) The first man to live on earth was 969 years old. This man was called Noah. True or false?

(14) The first man who walked with God, and he did not die. What was his name?

(15) The first man that was taken up into heaven by God during his faithful journey on earth was called Moses.
True or false?

(16) The first ship that sailed on the ocean during the flood. Who was the captain of that ship (the Ark)?

(17) The first skyscraper ever constructed in the Bible was remembered by what name, and in what city was it constructed?

(18) The first person to be turned into a pillar of salt. Whose wife was she?

(19) The first city that was destroyed before the flood and by whom?

(20) The first man that God tested to kill his son. What was the name of that man?

(21) The first wedding veil that was worn by a woman. Who was the woman?

(22) The first time "two nations" were in a woman's womb. What was the name of that mother?

(23) The first time a brother sold his "birthright." That person was called Daniel. True or false?

(24) The first man that wrestled with an angel. What was his name?

(25) The first ladder that stretched from heaven to earth. Who had that dream about that ladder?

(26) The first coat that was made with many colors. The owner of that coat was called Elijah.
True or false?

(27) The first Hebrew boy who was made governor over Egypt by Pharaoh was called David.
True or false?

(28) The very first time that Joseph the dreamer wept. In what country, and why did he weep?

(29) The first time a new Pharaoh who knew not Joseph. Why?

(30) The first baby boy to sail on the river. What was his name?

(31) The first bush that burned but was not consumed. Who was this man that saw the bush burning?

(32) The first time God made Moses Pharaoh's God. When, and where did this happen?

(33) The ten destructive "Plagues of Egypt" was done by Adam and Eve. True or false?

(34) God's great "miracle" at the Red Sea for the Israelites. Who was their leader at that time?

(35) The first song that was sung after crossing over. Who all sang this new song?

(36) The children of Israel first murmured against Moses. Where and why did it happen?

(37) The first table of stone (the Ten Commandments) was written by whose finger? Was it Moses or Aaron?
True or false?

(38) The first time Aaron made gods (molten calf) for the children of Israel to worship. Name the place, the time, and why Aaron did it.

(39) The first time the children of Israel were called "a stiff-necked people." By whom?

(40) The first food that was dropped from heaven for the children of Israel to eat was dropped by Moses. True or false?

(41) The first time Moses broke the table of stone, which was given to him by God. Why did Moses do that?
Was Moses hungry or just happy?

(42) The first time God killed 3,000 Israelites for disobedience. Where, and when did this happen?

(43) The first time the Ark of God was brought into the tabernacle. By whom?

(44) The first sin offering, peace offering, trespass offering, etc., of the tabernacle was done by Jacob and Eusa. True or false?

(45) The first time all baby boys were circumcised on the eighth day after birth. In what chapter of the Bible was this found?

(46) The first time several men were sent to search Canaan, "the land of milk and honey." Name the leader who sent these men.

(47) The first time "giants and grasshoppers" were heard. Who said those words, and why?

(48) The first man who was put to death for breaking the "Sabbath law." Name the book of the Bible where it was recorded.

(49) The first group of rebels was in the Bible. Name the chapter of the Bible.

(50) The first coup d'état on the face of the earth that failed. Where did this happen, and why?

(51) The first time the earth opened her mouth and swallowed some Israelites alive. Name the chapter of the Bible where it is recorded.

(52) The first time the river of Jordan was divided and rose upon a heap for the children of Israel to cross over.
Who was their leader when this happened? Was it David, Moses, or Joshua?

(53) The first time the wall of Jericho fell down flat, and how many times the children of Israel went around the wall before the wall of Jericho came down?

(54) The first king of Israel was called Saul. True or false?

(55) The youngest king of Israel was seven years old. What was his name?

(56) The first king of Israel who was rejected by God. That king was Solomon. True or false?

(57) The first spaceship that traveled into space with only one astronomer on board. That astronomer was called Elijah. True or false?

(58) The first submarine to travel under the water for three days in the Bible, with only one sailor on board in a belly of big fish. What was the name of that sailor?

(59) The first time a group of hungry lions in their den refused to eat their dinner. Who was that godly man who was in the lions' den at dinnertime?

(60) The first little shepherd boy who killed a giant of the Philistines called Goliath was David. True or false?

(61) The first time the "fiery furnace" could not consume the Hebrew boys. What were the names of the three Hebrew boys in the furnace?

(62) The first king of Israel who visited a witch doctor. Who was he, and why did he do this evil thing?

(63) The first "riddle" of Sampson. What was Sampson's wife called at the time of his riddle?

(64) The wisest king of Israel was called King Solomon. True or false?

(65) The first king of Israel that had seven hundred wives, princesses, and three hundred concubines. Who was that king of Israel?

(66) The first time a king of Israel refused to kill his enemy on two separate occasions because they both were the Lord's anointed. That king was David. True or false?

(67) The first king of Israel who ate the Lord's "hallowed bread" because he was hungry. What was the name of that king?

## The New Testament

(1) The very first virgin mother with a child called Jesus was Sarah. True or false?

(2) The first gifts that were brought to baby Jesus by the wise men were gold, frankincense, and myrrh. How many wise men were they?

(3) The first time Joseph, the father of Jesus, escaped into Egypt with his wife, Mary, and their child, Jesus, because King Herod wanted to kill Jesus. Who advised Joseph in a dream to escape into Egypt?

(4) The very first time a little child at twelve years old taught in the temple. What was the name of that child?

(5) The first time a man of God met Jesus, he baptized Him. Name that man of God.

(6) The very first time when Jesus was tempted by the devil, He said unto him: "Get thee hence, Satan." Name the location of his temptation.

(7) The first person on earth to feed 5,000 persons with five loaves of bread and two fishes was Peter. True or false?

(8) The first man in the Bible to say: "Follow me." Who was that man?

(9) The first miracle of turning water into wine was done by whom and where?

(10) The first man on earth that ordered the wind to "be still." And the wind obeyed him. That person's name was called Peter. True or false?

(11) The first servant of God who walked upon the water. Who was that person?

(12) The first person who raised a dead man from the grave. What was the name of the dead man?

(13) The very first time that a man of God said, "Let the dead bury the dead" was said by Peter. True or false?

(14) The first disciple who said, "Lord, it is good to be here." That disciple's name was James. True or false?

(15) The first man of God that said, "Take up your bed and walk." At what place did it happen, and who was the man of God?

(16) The first woman with an issue of blood for twelve years was healed by Prophet Elisha. True or false?

(17) He said for the very first time, "Come down from the sycamore tree." What was the name of the man who was up in the tree?

(18) The first man that cursed the fig tree was called James. True or false?

(19) The first time a man of God said, "Let him without sin cast the first stone." The man of God was Jesus.
True or false?

(20) The first time a man of God was questioned by the elders and the priest about His authority. Name the man of God.

(21) A servant of God who drove the moneychangers from the temple for the first time. Who was that servant of God?

(22) The first man of God that spoke about a "Good Samaritan." Who was that man?

(23) The first time a servant of God said, "One of you will betray me." Name the servant of God who said those words.

(24) The first time that the "Last Supper" was held, and by whom?

(25) The first time that Jesus said to one of His disciples, "When the cock crows, you will deny me twice." Name the disciple.

(26) The first time a servant of God rode into Jerusalem for the last time on a donkey. That man of God was Matthew. True or false?

(27) The first and the last kiss that betrayed Jesus before his death. Name the betrayer.

(28) The first disciple of Jesus that hung himself. That disciple's name was Peter. True or false?

(29) The seven words on the cross were said for the first and the last time by whom?

(30) The first servant of God who death could not keep in the grave. Name that servant.

(31) The first servant of God who rose from the dead within three days. What was the name of God's servant?

(32) The first two women who saw Jesus after His resurrection from the dead were called Hannah and Rebecca. True or false?

(33) The first time Jesus said, "Touch me not; for I am not yet ascended to my Father." When did Jesus say those words?

(34) The first time Jesus said, after His resurrection, "I am hungry." Name the place, and who did Jesus ask for the food?

(35) The first and the last time that Jesus ascended into heaven. Name what books of the Bible it was recorded in.

(36) The first time that Jesus' disciples were at one accord when they all were filled with the Holy Ghost and began to speak with other tongues. When did this happen? In what book of the Bible is it found?

## THE LAST DAYS

**Christian brothers and sisters, I personally believe that we are presently living in the last days of our lives. Jesus could come back any second, minute, hour, day, week, month, or year. Are you as a true believer of Christ ready to receive Him when He comes?**

Take a glance and just look all around you. Strange things are happening daily like wars with nations against nations, kingdoms against kingdoms, and earthquakes; unexplained fire, floods, pestilence, etc., occurring all over the world.

Children and parents are against one another, brothers against brothers. Families are also against families. False prophets, false Christs, corruption, persecution and execution of Christians, human trafficking, slavery, sexual abuse, the displacement of hundreds of thousands of people all over the world; drugs, homosexuality, poverty, criminality—you name it—it's happening.

Remember that Jesus said that most of those things would happen during the last days before the end of time (Matthew 24:1–51). Also, Jesus informed us that the Gospel will be preached to the whole world before He comes.

In my opinion, the Gospel has already been preached throughout the whole world (Matthew 24:1–14; Luke 21:1–18).

Remember that Christ said, **"Heaven and earth shall pass away, but my words shall not pass away"** (Matthew 24:34–35; Luke 21:32–33 kjv).

Believers of Christ, "The day and hour of the coming of the Lord knoweth no man; not even the angels of heaven, but my Father only," Jesus said (Matthew 24:36–37 kjv). The Lord shall come in a day when His servant looketh not for Him; and in an hour that he is not aware of (Matthew 24:50–51 kjv). Every eye shall behold him, Christian friends, I believe. For example, there will be two women grinding at the mill; one shall be taken away, and the other left alone. Also, there shall be two persons working in the field, but only one will be taken away, and the other person left alone (Matthew 24:40–41 nkjv).

## CHRIST WILL SEPARATE THE SHEEP FROM THE GOATS

Brethren, Christ shall separate the people from one another, as a shepherd divideth his sheep from the goats. Also, the Lord shall set the sheep on the right hand, but the goats on the left, because I believe that no servant can serve two masters; for either he will hate the one, and love the other. Or else that person will despise the other; but you cannot serve God and mammon (Luke 16:10–13 kjv). Therefore, watch out, my dear brothers and sisters, because you know not what hour your Lord will come (Matthew 24:42–43 niv). Nevertheless, the Son of Man shall come in His glory and He shall come in the cloud with all the holy angels with Him; then shall He sit upon the throne of His glory (Matthew 25:31–32 kjv).

My dear beloved brethren, please ask yourself one last question: which side are you on today . . . the right side or the left side? You are either a goat or you are a sheep, because there is no animal on earth that God created called "goat-sheep." Therefore, you either serve God or Satan. The law of science teaches us that two things can't occupy the same space at the same time; this is called **"Impenetrability."** Remember that the good Lord said, **"Behold, I come quickly,"** saying of

**the prophecy of the book; and "behold, I come quickly, and my reward is with me, to give every man according as his work shall be."**

"I am Alpha and Omega; the Beginning and the End; the First and the Last." Amen, Amen, and Amen, in Jesus' name, Amen. Praise His holy name, because Jesus is the King of kings, and Lord of lords.

## A BIBLICAL QUIZ THROUGH YOUR JOURNEY WITH GOD

Finally, before I bring those **"very first few events of the Bible"** to a close, please be reminded, believers of Christ, that you will surely study the Overview of the Old and the New Testaments before you start your *Daily Journey With God Through The Year.* Recall that the Old Testament predicts the coming of the MESSIAH, whereas the New Testament unfolds God's promised coming of the MESSIAH. As you continue reading the Bible, you must study, search, and write down the answers to those questions which were previously listed regarding **"a glance at a few events of the Bible."** This Bible research will serve as a workshop/study guide as you travel through your *Daily Journey With God.* Also, Christian brethren, this will be your very first **biblical quiz** while you are traveling on this great journey. Notwithstanding, you will also be our own professor, as well as grading your test paper. I hope and pray that you will be truthful to yourself while answering and grading your paper, the end of your journey. Upon the completion of your **biblical quiz and grading,** just tell the Lord what grade you have given yourself, on your first quiz, what your grade will be. Will your grade be an A, B, C, D, or F? Believers of Christ, only you can answer this question. Lastly, while traveling on your daily journey with the Lord, you are advised to pray, fast, and to also write down a few notes. Most importantly, please write down your **prayer request** for the Lord in order for you to receive an answer to your prayers from **the powerhouse of God** very quickly. May the good Lord continue to bless you, and I pray for His light to forever shine upon you and give you peace, in Jesus' name, amen!

## PRAISE GOD FROM WHOM ALL BLESSINGS FLOW

I praise the Almighty God from whom all blessings flow. I thank God for the many sleepless nights I spent in writing *A Daily Journey With God Through The Year,* including **these great events of the Bible,** which I studied. I also praise God for the patience, wisdom, knowledge, and understanding He has given unto me to do His work.

Therefore, I praise God, Alleluia! I praise God, Amen; I praise God, Alleluia! And I praise God, Amen.

"Praise ye the Lord. Praise God in His sanctuary, praise God in the firmament of His Power. Praise Him for His mighty acts, praise Him according to His excellent greatness.

Praise Him with the sound of the trumpet; praise Him with the psaltery and harp.

Praise Him with the timbrel, and dance. Praise Him with stringed instruments, and organs.

Praise Him upon the loud cymbals; praise Him upon the high sounding cymbals.

**Let everything that hath breath praise the Lord. Praise ye the Lord!"** Amen! (Psalm 150:1–6 kjv)

## SUMMARY

The Old Testament predicts the coming of the MESSIAH, whereas the New Testament is the fulfillment of God's promises regarding the birth of Jesus Christ.

## AN OVERVIEW OF THE OLD TESTAMENT

**As you undertake *A Daily Journey With God Through The Year*, you will definitely study and learn that the Old Testament** predicts the coming of **Christ**. Those servants of God who wrote the scriptures regarding the coming of the **Messiah** were all faithful servants of God, who loved the Lord with all their heart, soul, and mind. Their faith was inspiring, and their commitment was motivating, because their predictions of the coming of **Messiah** were motivated by the inspiration of **God**, I strongly believe.

Remember, Christian friends, **God** is the same **God** of yesterday and today; He is a true and a living **God** that never fails. The Lord said, "for I am the Lord, I will speak, and the word that I shall speak shall come to pass" (Ezekiel 12:25 kjv).

## THE COMING OF THE MESSIAH

Because of **Adam** and **Eve's** sins, **Christ** had to come and to die for our sins that we too might be freed. Therefore, believers of Christ, before undertaking your ***Daily Journey With God Through***

*The Year,* you must first reflect on the **Overview of the Old Testament** concerning the coming of the Lord, Jesus Christ, the **MESSIAH.** "The Lord himself shall give you a sign; Behold a virgin shall conceive, and bear a son, and shall call his name Immanuel" (Isaiah 7:14 kjv). "But he was wounded for our transgressions, he was bruised for our iniquities; the chastisement of our peace was upon him, and with his stripes we are healed" (Isaiah 53:5 kjv). "I gave my back to the smiters, and my cheeks to them that plucked off my hair, I hid not my face from shame, and spitting" (Isaiah 50:6 kjv). "And after threescore and two weeks, shall the **Messiah** be cut off, but not for himself; and the people of the prince that shall come, shall destroy the city, and the sanctuary, and the end thereof shall be with a flood, and unto the end of the war desolations are determined" (Daniel 9:26 kjv). "I will pour upon the **House of David**, and upon the inhabitants of Jerusalem, the spirit of grace and of supplications and they shall look upon me whom they have pieced, and they shall mourn for him, as one mourneth for his only son, and shall be in bitterness, for his firstborn" (Zechariah 12:10 kjv).

Therefore, during *A Daily Journey With God Through The Year,* the Old Testament will teach you that the "his sons came to honor, and **he** knoweth it not; and they are brought low, but **he** perceiveth it not of them" (Job 14:21 kjv). "Before the Lord: for **he** cometh, for **he** cometh to judge the earth: **he** shall judge the world with righteousness, and the people with the truth" (Psalm 96:13 kjv). "But thou, Bethlehem Ephratah, though thou be little among the thousands of **Judah**, yet out of thee shall **he** come forth unto me that is to be **ruler** in **Israel**; whose goings forth have been from of old, from everlasting" (Micah 5:2 kjv).

The Old Testament further explained that "The Lord thy **God** will raise up unto thee a **Prophet** from the midst of thee, of thy brethren, like unto me; unto him ye shall hearken" (Deuteronomy 18:15 kjv). While you are undertaking this daily journey, the Old Testament will also narrate to you, that, "For unto us a child is born, unto us a **son** is given: and the government shall be upon his shoulder: and his name shall be called **Wonderful, Counsellor, The mighty God, The everlasting Father, The Prince of Peace"** (Isaiah 9:6 kjv). "Rejoice greatly, O daughter of Zion; shout, O daughter of Jerusalem: behold, thy King cometh unto thee: he is just, and having **salvation;** lowly, and **riding** upon an ass, and upon a colt the foal of an ass." Amen! (Zechariah 9:9 kjv)

## GOD'S CREATION

**The Old Testament** traced **God's** plan from the beginning of his **CREATION** unto the sixth day, when God said, "Let **us** make man in **our** own image, after **our** likeness: and let them have dominion over the fish of the sea, and over the fowl of the air, and over the cattle, and over all the earth, and over every creeping thing that creepeth upon the earth." **After the completion of God's work on the sixth day, He rested on the seventh day. Therefore, God blessed the seventh day, and sanctified it** (Genesis 1:26; Genesis 2:1–3 kjv).

Fortunately, believers of Christ, it was predicted in the **Old Testament** that **Christ** must come to die for the sin of **Adam** and **Eve,** that we too might live. Also, as you walk through your ***Daily Journey With God,*** you will study in the **Old Testament** about the **flood of Noah,** including God's covenant to **Abraham, Isaac, and Jacob** regarding the **Promised Land** which flows with milk and honey. You also will learn how God tested **Abraham** with his only son, **Isaac**; and later, **Rebecca,** the wife of **Isaac,** was mentioned in the Bible with **"two nations"** in her womb. The Bible also reminds us how **Esau** sold his **birthright** to his brother **Jacob**, and gives an account of the reconciliation of the two brothers, **Jacob and Esau**, at a later date. **The Old Testament** also teaches us how **Jacob's** name was changed by God to **"Israel,"** and that the twelve tribes of Israel was from the house of **Jacob (Israel).** We further studied about Joseph's coat of many colors that he wore when he was sold by his brothers for twenty pieces of silver because of his many dreams. Fortunately, Joseph was made the governor of Egypt by Pharaoh, because he was blessed by **God** from the beginning of his life. Joseph finally brought all of his brothers, including his father, to Egypt to live with him, where he cared and nourished them daily. Unfortunately, there came a new Pharaoh of Egypt at a later date that knew not Joseph.

## THE CHILDREN OF ISRAEL IN BONDAGE

Believers of Christ, whenever you are undertaking ***A Daily Journey With God Through The Year,*** please note that the Old Testament will explain to you how the children of Israel cried unto the Lord to deliver them from bondage. The good Lord answered their prayers by calling Moses from the "burning bush," who led his people out of bondage, after being in Egypt for 430 years. And it came to pass that Pharaoh refused to let the children of Israel go to serve the Lord in the wilderness as requested by Moses and Aaron, the servants of the true and the living God. Nevertheless, after so many plagues that were placed upon Egypt by the Lord, Pharaoh finally agreed to let the children go, after the tenth plague, but it was too late. This tenth plague that came upon Egypt from God was the death of all the firstborn sons of Egypt, including Pharaoh's own son whom he loved so dearly, I believe (Exodus 3:1–22; Exodus 4:1–31; Exodus 5:1–23; Exodus 6:1–30; etc. kjv).

## AT THE RED SEA

Unfortunately, and immediately after the children of Israel had left Egypt for the very first time after being in bondage for 430 years, Pharaoh had a change of heart, and he decided to chase after God's people in the wilderness. Because of the Lord's great miracle at the Red Sea, Pharaoh's army was overthrown and drown in the Red Sea. After crossing the Red Sea, God **FED** the children of Israel with food dropped directly from heaven, but the Israelites were very disobedient and rebellious; as a result, Moses broke the first two tablets of testimony, which were written with God's finger. It will be recalled when Moses came down from Mount Sinai after receiving the Ten Commandments from God, the children of Israel were worshiping a false god (a golden calf). Moses' anger waxed hot because of those "stiff-necked" people, the children of Israel, that caused him to break the first Ten Commandments which were given unto him by God (Exodus 14:1–31; Exodus 32: 1–35 kjv).

## MOSES STRUCK THE ROCK

Unfortunately, the Old Testament informed us that Moses didn't enter the Promised Land, as he had anticipated, because he struck the rock to obtain water for the Israelites to drink in disobedience to God. However, as you continue your ***Daily Journey With God Through The Year,*** you will discover how God showed Moses the Promised Land. He viewed it, but he never entered it. Upon the death of Moses, Joshua succeeded him as the new leader of the children of Israel. It should be recalled, God instructed Moses to speak to the rock at Kadesh, and the water would flow out of it; instead, Moses disobeyed God by striking the rock, because he was angry with the children of Israel. The Old Testament tells us that the children of Israel did lots of evil in the sight of the Lord; thus, God sold them to their enemies, and later on, the good Lord forgave them of their sins and rescued them. In the Bible, we also studied about the army of Gideon, as well as Samson and Delilah, and Ruth and Naomi.

## THE FIRST KING OF ISRAEL

Christian brothers and sisters, as you undertake ***A Daily Journey With God Through The Year,*** the Bible will teach you how God anointed Saul as the very first king of Israel, but he was later rejected by God because of disobedience. Recall that Samuel, the prophet, said unto King Saul, for the very first, and the last, time, "to obey is better than sacrifice, and to hearken than the fat of rams. For rebellion is as the sin of witchcraft, and stubbornness is as iniquity and idolatry. Because thou hast rejected the word of the Lord, he hath also rejected thee from being king" (1 Samuel 15:22–27 kjv).

Fortunately, David was crowned the next king of Israel, at the age of thirty years old, replacing King Saul. David was a very good king, a man after God's own heart. King David also loved the Lord. Unfortunately, the downfall of David was when he had Uriah killed on the battlefield, and then he took Bathsheba, the wife of Uriah, as his wife. After the death of King David, the Old Testament tells us that Solomon, his son, succeeded his father David, as king of Israel. King Solomon was the wisest man that ever lived, but his 700 wives and princesses, including his 300 concubines, turned his heart from God. There were other kings of Israel after the death of King Solomon, but just a few of them loved God as their father King David did. The majority of those kings of Israel did evil in the sight of God. As a result, the good Lord punished them for their sins, and He also divided their kingdom among their enemies.

In the Old Testament, we also studied about Elijah and the 450 false Baal prophets. We also studied about Elisha, who succeeded the prophet Elijah. As you continue your ***Daily Journey With God Through The Year***, you will study about King Hezekiah, Queen Vashti, and Queen Esther, as well as a great faithful servant of God who was called Job. Brethren, before you come to the end of your study, you will notice that the Old Testament will definitely teach you about the Psalms of David, the book of Proverbs, the Song of Solomon, as well as other great books of the Bible. **Additionally, some of God's great prophets in the Old Testament that you will also study are Eli, Samuel, Nathan, Isaiah, Jeremiah, Ezekiel, Daniel, Jonah, Malachi,** etc.

**FINALLY, THE OVERVIEW OF THE OLD TESTAMENT** is very important to us, Christian friends, as we undertake our study because it will bring us closer to God as we delve into His Word; and it will also strengthen our **faith** in the Lord, because it predicts the coming of the **Messiah.** Amen.

## AN OVERVIEW OF THE NEW TESTAMENT

Believers of Christ, as you undertake ***A DAILY JOURNEY WITH GOD THROUGH THE YEAR,*** it is important that you realize that the New Testament unfolds God's promises in the Old Testament regarding the prediction of the coming of the MESSIAH in the books of: Genesis, Deuteronomy, Job, Psalms, Isaiah, Daniel, Zechariah, and others.

While you are studying the New Testament, you will recall what the good Lord said, "For God so loved the world, that he gave his only begotten Son, that whosoever believed in him should not perish, but have everlasting life" (John 3:16 kjv). Remember, Christian friends, as you walk through your daily journey with God, please read carefully what the Bible tells you about the Lord: "The Lord thy God, He is God, a faithful God which keepeth His covenant and mercy with them that love Him. The Lord keeps His commandments to a thousand of generations" (Deuteronomy 7:9 kjv).

Recall in Old Testament that the Bible taught us that God kept His covenant with Abraham, Isaac, and Jacob as He did in the New Testament with the coming and fulfillment of Christ the Messiah. God always keeps His promises, because He never fails. Therefore, brethren, "For God sent not his Son into the world to condemn the world; but that the world through him might be saved" (John 3:17 kjv). "She shall bring forth a son, and thou shall call his name Jesus: for he shall save his people from their sins" (Matthew 1:21 kjv).

## BETHLEHEM, THE BIRTH PLACE OF CHRIST THE MESSIAH

Christian brothers and sisters, while you are undertaking *A Daily Journey With God Through The Year,* please remember that Christ was born in Bethlehem of Judea. Recall that in the days of Herod the king, behold there came wise men from the east to Jerusalem on **"their journey,"** and they said, "Where is he that is born King of the Jews? for we have seen his star in the east and have come to worship him. However, when King Herod heard these things, he was troubled, and all Jerusalem with him" (Matthew 2:1–3 kjv).

## KING HEROD TO WORSHIP JESUS?

No! King Herod had bad intentions about worshiping Jesus. He wanted to kill baby Jesus instead of worshipping Him, because the Bible said, **"A Governor shall rule my people, Israel"** (Matthew 2:6 kjv). I strongly believe King Herod was thinking within his heart that Jesus was coming to overthrow him and to take away his kingdom on earth, so Herod was very afraid of baby Jesus.

King Herod was wrong, because Jesus was born unto the Virgin Mary for a special mission on earth to die for our sins. His kingdom was not of this earth; instead, Jesus' kingdom is in heaven; where His spiritual Father is. It must be recalled that King Herod said earlier in this scripture, when he was informed by the wise men about the birth of Jesus, "Where is he that is born King of the Jews? for we have seen his star in the east, and have come to worship him" (Matthew 2:1–2 kjv).

## THE THREE WISE MEN

Then Herod privately called the wise men and inquired of them diligently what time the star appeared. He then sent the wise men on a "special spy mission" to Bethlehem, and he said unto them: "Go and search diligently for the young child; and when ye have found him, bring me word again, that I may come and worship him also" (Matthew 2:8 kjv). Thus, on their journey to search for baby Jesus, the three wise men followed the "star," and they rejoiced with exceeding great joy when they found baby Jesus with His mother, Mary, and Joseph, His father. The wise men fell down on their face and worshipped Him, and they presented baby Jesus with gifts: gold, frankincense, and myrrh. Being warned by God in a dream, the wise men didn't return to Herod as anticipated by him; instead, they went another way, returning to their own country (Matthew 2:1–12 kjv).

## AN ESCAPE TO EGYPT FOR SAFETY

The New Testament tells us an angel of the Lord appeared unto Joseph in a dream: "that he must arise, and take the young child and his mother, Mary; and flee into Egypt, for Herod will seek the young child to destroy him." Joseph immediately took the family to Egypt, as instructed by God until the death of King Herod (Matthew 2:13–17 nkjv).

Understandably, the trip to Egypt was very frightening, and a long, lonesome journey undertaken by Joseph, and his family, I strongly believe. Nevertheless, this was a fulfillment that was spoken of the Lord's prophet, saying, "Out of Egypt have I called my son" (Matthew 2:15 kjv). Unfortunately, Herod killed all the male children that were in Bethlehem, from two years old and under, because the wise men mocked him in searching for baby Jesus to have him killed (Matthew 2:15–23 kjv). I also believe that Herod was a very wicked king.

## "FEAR NOT, MARY"

Christian friends, whenever you are undertaking your **Daily Journey With God Through The Year**, remember that an angel of the Lord said unto Mary, **"Fear not, Mary, for thou hast found favor with God. And behold, thou shall conceive in thy womb, and bring forth a Son, and shall call His name Jesus. For He shall be great, and He shall be called the Son of**

**the highest, and the Lord God shall give unto Him the throne of His father David"** (Luke 1:23–32 kjv). It must be recalled the in the sixth month, the angel Gabriel was sent from God unto a city called Nazareth, to a virgin woman called Mary, the wife of Joseph, from the house of David, because the good Lord favored Mary (Luke 1:26–27 kjv).

## GOD'S FULFILLMENT OF THE MESSIAH

Believers of Christ, the New Testament is the fulfillment of the birth of CHRIST, the MESSIAH, who is the Son of David, according to the prophets of the Old Testament. Recall that the prophet Isaiah said, "Therefore, the Lord himself shall give you a sign, behold a virgin shall conceive; and bear a Son and shall call His name Immanuel. For unto us a child is born, unto us a son is given: and the government shall be upon his shoulder: and his name shall be called Wonderful, Counsellor, The mighty God, The everlasting Father, The Prince of Peace." While you are on your ***Daily Journey With God Through The Year***, please bear in mind, believer of Christ, that JESUS was wounded for our transgressions. He was also bruised for our iniquities, the chastisement of our peace was upon Him, and with His stripes, we are healed. The prophet Isaiah continued, **"I gave my back to the smiters, and my cheeks to them that plucked off the hair: I hid not my face from shame and spitting"**; (Isaiah 50:6 kjv).

## THE GENERATION OF JESUS CHRIST

Therefore, brethren, as you continue your ***Daily Journey With God Through The Year***, please be reminded that the New Testament traced the generation of Jesus Christ directly to the Son of David, the Son of Abraham, as follows: "The book of the generation of Jesus Christ, the Son of David the Son of Abraham; Abraham begat Isaac, Isaac begat Jacob, Jacob begat Judas, and his brethren; Eliud begat Eleazar, Eleazar begat Mattan, Mattan begat Jacob. Jacob begat Joseph, the husband of Mary, whom was born Jesus, who is called Christ. Nevertheless, all the generations from Abraham to David are fourteen generations; and from David until the carrying away into Babylon are fourteen generations" (Matthew 1:1–17 kjv).

## JESUS HAD THREE DIFFERENT FATHERS

According to the Bible, Jesus had three different fathers, and their names are as follows: God, His Heavenly Father, and His two earthly fathers were David the son of Jesse, and Joseph the husband of Mary, who is the mother of Jesus.

As you walk through *A Daily Journey With God Through The Year*, you will recall that Jesus was originally in heaven before God's creation, and He was later sent down to earth by God to save us from our sins. Remember, when God said in the beginning on the sixth day of His creation: "Let US make man in OUR image, after OUR likeness: and let them have dominion over the fish of the sea, and over the fowl of the air, and over the cattle, and over all the earth, and over every creeping thing that creepeth upon the earth" (Genesis 1:26 kjv). On the **sixth day of God's creation, He used the words "US" and "OUR," referring to the "TRI–UNITY," which is called the "TRINITY"** by Christians all over the world.

Please be reminded, Christian friends, the word **"TRINITY"** is not mentioned in the Bible according to my research, but God the Father, God the Son, and God the Holy Spirit are mentioned in the Bible. Therefore, I strongly believed that Jesus was a part of God's CREATION in the BEGINNING, because God used the words "US" and "OUR", referring to Jesus the Son, and the Holy Spirit, including God Himself. According to the New Testament, God the Father is the ultimate source of the UNIVERSE, and He is also an AUTHORITY over Jesus. Jesus is the Son of God, as well as a special "AGENT" of the Father who takes orders directly from God, but the Holy Spirit is where God creates and maintains the UNIVERSE, I believe.

Recall that Jesus is the "SEED" of David, a direct descendant of Abraham, and David the Son of Jesse, and Joseph the husband of Mary, who is the mother of Jesus. Therefore, Jesus said, "I AM" the "ROOT," the offspring of David. The prophecies of the Bible must be fulfilled, amen

## THAT OLD RUGGED CROSS OF CALVARY

Recall that Jesus had a very busy schedule and a **"long, lonesome journey"** while he was on earth. He taught in the temple at the age of twelve years old, and He later selected His twelve disciples to assist Him in carrying out God's work. Jesus also taught in the synagogues, preaching the gospel of the kingdom, and healing all manners of diseases and sickness among the people. Jesus also took "a short journey" as He walked on the sea for the very first time, my beloved brethren. Then, Jesus finally took the most **"lonesome and painful journey"** during His final hours on earth, when those wicked Roman soldiers made Him carry His own cross on which to be crucified. Brethren, as we undertake *A Daily Journey With God Through The Year*, we must always remember that Christ died on **"THAT OLD RUGGED CROSS"** of Calvary, where He shed His **BLOOD** for our sins, that we too might live.

## THE BEATITUDES

The New Testament taught us that Jesus went up into a mountain, along with His disciples during one of His **"early journeys on earth,"** and a multitude of people came to Him to hear His teaching. Jesus taught them, and He blessed the poor in spirit, including those who were mourning their loved ones. He blessed the meek, for they shall inherit the earth; and Jesus blessed those that were hungry and thirsty for righteousness, for they shall be satisfied. Jesus also blessed the merciful, because they shall obtain mercy, including the pure in heart, for they shall see God. He blessed the peacemakers, for they shall be called the children of God. Jesus blessed those who were persecuted for the sake of righteousness, for theirs is the kingdom of heaven. Amen!

## THE KINGDOM OF HEAVEN

More importantly, as you travel on your *Daily Journey With God Through The Year,* we will study how Jesus taught the people about the Kingdom of Heaven before His death. Jesus said unto them, "Let not your heart be troubled: ye believe in God, believe also in me. In my Father's house are many mansions: if it were not so, I would have told you. I go to prepare a place for you. I will come again, and receive you unto myself; that where I am, there ye may be also" (John 14:1–3, KJV).

## THE CURSE IS LIFTED

Believers of Christ, while you are undertaking your *Daily Journey With God Through The Year,* please remember that Jesus paid the price for all of our sins when He shed His blood, and He was crucified on that **"Old Rugged Cross of Calvary."** Therefore, the **curse is lifted** regarding the sins of **mankind.** All we have to do as Christians is to **look up** to the **Cross of Calvary**, because "death" just could not keep Jesus in the grave; instead, He is risen, and He is alive, and Jesus will definitely come again to take us with Him into heaven

## A GLANCE AT A FEW ACCOMPLISHMENTS AND MIRACLES OF JESUS ON EARTH

Christian friends, as you come to the end of ***A Daily Journey With God Through The Year,*** please remember a few of Jesus' **accomplishments and miracles** while He was on earth. Some are as follows:

### A Few Of Jesus' Accomplishment

- Jesus never sinned.
- Jesus died for the sins of all mankind.
- Jesus fulfilled dozens of prophecies.
- Jesus taught mankind how to relate to God.
- Jesus started His first teaching in the temple at the age of twelve years old.
- Jesus cared for the poor and the sick.
- Jesus carried His own cross on His shoulder on his way to be crucified.
- Jesus trained His disciples, and He taught the people about the Kingdom of God.
- Jesus spoke in many parables.
- Death could not keep Him in the grave.
- Jesus was resurrected from the dead.

### A Few Of Jesus' Miracles

- Jesus turned water into wine, his very first miracle (John 2:1–11).
- Jesus cured the nobleman's son (John 4:46–47).
- Jesus cast out an unclean spirit (Mark 1:23–28).
- Jesus walked on water (Matthew 14:25–36).
- Jesus instructs His disciples to haul fish from the water (Luke 5:1–11).
- Jesus healed the leper (Mark 1:40–45).

- Jesus cured Peter's mother-in-law of a fever (Mark 1:30–31).
- Jesus raised a widow's son from the dead (Luke 7:11–18).
- Jesus healed the centurion's servant (a man under authority) (Matthew 8:5–13).
- Jesus commanded the wind to be still (Matthew 8:23–27).
- Jesus cured the paralytic (Matthew 9:1–8).
- Jesus fed 5,000 people with five loaves of bread and two fishes (Matthew 14:15–21).
- Jesus cured a deaf man (Mark 7:31–37).
- Jesus also fed a great multitude of 4,000 with seven loaves of bread and a few fishes (Matthew 15:32–39).
- Jesus cured a man of dropsy (Luke 14:1–14).
- Jesus opened the eyes of a man born blind (John 9:1–38).
- Jesus cleansed ten lepers (Luke 17:11–19).
- Jesus opened the eyes of two blind men (Matthew 20:30–34).
- Jesus caused the fig tree to wither away (Mark 11:12–14).
- Jesus instructs His disciples for the second time to fish in the sea for a great catch (John 21:1–14).
- Jesus restored the ear of the high priest's servant (Luke 22:50–51).
- Jesus cured all manner of diseases and sicknesses of the people.
- Finally, DEATH just could not keep Jesus in the grave; instead, He ROSE from the dead (Luke 24:1–7).

Therefore, Christian brothers and sisters, you need to always remember that Christ died for our sins. As you conclude ***A DAILY JOURNEY WITH GOD THROUGH THE YEAR***, just keep in mind that Jesus loves you, and He is risen, and He will surely come again (John 14:1–4). **PRAISE THE LORD!**

# 3 A Daily Journey With God Through The Year

## (A letter to the readers)

Dear Believers of Christ,

Before undertaking your spiritual journey with God this New Year, you must first invoke the presence of the Lord so that you may be guided by the Holy Spirit. You must listen attentively for the voice of the Lord by being obedient and also keep silent before Him in order for you to hear a special message from the Lord, because when the "Lord is in His Holy Temple, let all the earth be silent before Him." For the Lord God Almighty instructed His children to memorize and to meditate on His Word so that they can accurately answer questions. Christian friends, while you are on your daily journey with God, you must also encourage others to take up their cross and follow Him in winning souls for Christ. May the grace of God guide and strengthen you on your journey. Please continue to stay blessed. Amen!

Elder Charles B. Harris Sr.

A Daily Journey with God Through the Year

| | | | |
|---|---|---|---|
| 1. | God's Creation | Genesis 1–2 | January 1 |
| 2. | The First Wedding | Genesis 3–5 | January 2 |
| 3. | God Repented | Genesis 6–9 | January 3 |
| 4. | The First Skyscraper | Genesis 10–11 | January 4 |

| | | | |
|---|---|---|---|
| 5. | Abram Leaves His Father's House | Genesis 12–14 | January 5 |
| 6. | God's First Covenant with Abram | Genesis 15–17 | January 6 |
| 7. | Fast, Pray, and Rest | -------------------- | January 7 |
| 8. | Sarah Lied to God | Genesis 18–20 | January 8 |
| 9. | God Tested Abraham's Faith | Genesis 21–24 | January 9 |
| 10. | Abraham Gave Up the Ghost | Genesis 25–26 | January 10 |
| 11. | Jacob Stole Esau's Blessing | Genesis 27–31 | January 11 |
| 12. | 12. Jacob and Esau Reconciled | Genesis 32–36 | January 12 |
| 13. | 13. Joseph's Coat of Many Colors | Genesis 37–40 | January 13 |
| 14. | 14. Fast, Pray, and Rest | -------------------- | January 14 |
| 15. | Pharaoh's Dream | Genesis 41–44 | January 15 |
| 16. | Joseph and His Brothers | Genesis 45–47 | January 16 |
| 17. | Israel Blessed Joseph's Two Sons | Genesis 48–50 | January 17 |
| 18. | A Pharaoh that Knew Not Joseph | Exodus 1–2 | January 18 |
| 19. | Moses and the Burning Bush | Exodus 3–6 | January 19 |
| 20. | The Lord Made Moses Pharaoh's God | Exodus 7–10 | January 20 |
| 21. | Fast, Pray, and Rest | -------------------- | January 21 |
| 22. | "When I See the Blood, I Will Pass over You" | Exodus 11–12 | January 22 |
| 23. | "Sanctify unto Me All the Firstborn" | Exodus 13–15 | January 23 |
| 24. | Manna (Bread) Rained from Heaven | Exodus 16–18 | January 24 |
| 25. | God Appeared on Mount Sinai | Exodus 19–20 | January 25 |
| 26. | The Ten Commandments | Exodus 21–24 | January 26 |
| 27. | The Lord's Tabernacle | Exodus 25–27 | January 27 |
| 28. | Fast, Pray, and Rest | -------------------- | January 28 |
| 29. | Holiness to the Lord | Exodus 28–31 | January 29 |
| 30. | Aaron, "Make Us Gods" | Exodus 32–34 | January 30 |
| 31. | The Sabbath Day | Exodus 35–40 | January 31 |
| 32. | Meat Offering and Peace Offering | Leviticus 1–3 | February 1 |
| 33. | Sin Offering and Trespass Offering | Leviticus 4–7 | February 2 |
| 34. | Moses Anointed Aaron | Leviticus 8–10 | February 3 |
| 35. | Clean and Uncleaned Meat | Leviticus 11–15 | February 4 |

| | | | |
|---|---|---|---|
| 65. | The Tribes' Land Inheritance | Joshua 18–21 | March 5 |
| 66. | The Last Words of Joshua | Joshua 22–24 | March 6 |
| 67. | Fast, Pray, and Rest | -------------------- | March 7 |
| 68. | 70 Kings' Thumbs and Toes Were Cut Off | Judges 1–5 | March 8 |
| 69. | The Children of Israel Did Evil | Judges 6–8 | March 9 |
| 70. | Gideon and the Lord | Judges 13–16 | March 10 |
| 71. | The Birth of Samson | Judges 13–16 | March 11 |
| 72. | The Death of Samson | Judges 17–21 | March 12 |
| 73. | "Thy God Will Be My God" | Ruth 1–4 | March 13 |
| 74. | Fast, Pray, and Rest | -------------------- | March 14 |
| 75. | Hannah's Vow to the Lord | 1 Samuel 1–3 | March 15 |
| 76. | The Death of Eli | 1 Samuel 4–8 | March 16 |
| 77. | Saul Anointed King of Israel | 1 Samuel 9–12 | March 17 |
| 78. | The Lord Rejected King Saul | 1 Samuel 13–15 | March 18 |
| 79. | Little Shepherd Boy Anointed King | 1 Samuel 16–19 | March 19 |
| 80. | David Eats the Lord's Hallowed Bread | 1 Samuel 20–23 | March 20 |
| 81. | Fast, Pray, and Rest | -------------------- | March 21 |
| 82. | David Took King Saul's Spear and Water | 1 Samuel 24–26 | March 22 |
| 83. | David into His Enemy's Territory | 1 Samuel 27–31 | March 23 |
| 84. | David Killed One of Saul's Men | 2 Samuel 1–4 | March 24 |
| 85. | David Anointed King of Israel | 2 Samuel 5–7 | March 25 |
| 86. | David Reigned over All Israel | 2 Samuel 8–10 | March 26 |
| 87. | The Downfall of King David | 2 Samuel 11–14 | March 27 |
| 88. | Fast, Pray, and Rest | -------------------- | March 28 |
| 89. | Absalom Wanted to Be King, but . . . | 2 Samuel 15–18 | March 29 |
| 90. | King David Maintained His Throne | 2 Samuel 19–20 | March 30 |
| 91. | David's Heart Acted Foolishly | 2 Samuel 21–24 | March 31 |
| 92. | The Death of King David | 1 Kings 1–4 | April 1 |
| 93. | King Solomon's Temple | 1 Kings 5–8 | April 2 |
| 94. | King Solomon's Downfall | 1 Kings 9–11 | April 3 |
| 95. | The Israelite's Civil War | 1 Kings 12–16 | April 4 |

| | | |
|---|---|---|
| 188. A Good Name Is Better Than Riches | Proverbs 22–24 | July 6 |
| 189. Fast, Pray, and Rest | -------------------- | July 7 |
| 190. The Wicked Flee, No Man Pursueth | Proverbs 25–29 | July 8 |
| 191. 1King Lemuel, the Prophecy | Proverbs 30–31 | July 9 |
| 192. To Every Thing, There Is a Season | Ecclesiastes 1–6 | July 10 |
| 193. A Good Name Is Better Than Precious Ointment | Ecclesiastes 7–12 | July 11 |
| 194. Solomon's Song | Song of Solomon 1–8 | July 12 |
| 195. The Vision of Isaiah | Isaiah 1–4 | July 13 |
| 196. Fast, Pray, and Rest | -------------------- | July 14 |
| 197. Holy, Holy, Holy Is the Lord of Hosts | Isaiah 5–8 | July 15 |
| 198. A Rod Out of the Stem of Jesse | Isaiah 9–1 | July 16 |
| 199. The Burden of Babylon | Isaiah 13–16 | July 17 |
| 200. The Burden of Damascus | Isaiah 17–20 | July 18 |
| 201. The Burden of the Desert | Isaiah 21–23 | July 19 |
| 202. O Lord, Thou Art God | Isaiah 24–27 | July 20 |
| 203. Fast, Pray, and Rest | -------------------- | July 21 |
| 204. Woe to the Crown of Pride | Isaiah 28–30 | July 22 |
| 205. Come Near, Ye Nations | Isaiah 31–35 | July 23 |
| 206. King Hezekiah's Illness | Isaiah 36–39 | July 24 |
| 207. But They That Wait upon the Lord | Isaiah 40–43 | July 25 |
| 208. "There Is No God Besides Me" | Isaiah 44–48 | July 26 |
| 209. Look unto Abraham Your Father | Isaiah 49–51 | July 27 |
| 210. Fast, Pray, and Rest | -------------------- | July 28 |
| 211. "Awake, Awake, Put on the Strength" | Isaiah 52–57 | July 29 |
| 212. Cry Aloud, Spare Not! | Isaiah 58–62 | July 30 |
| 213. "The Heaven Is My Throne" | Isaiah 63–66 | July 31 |
| 214. Circumcise Yourself to the Lord | Jeremiah 1–6 | August 1 |
| 215. The Words of the Lord to Jeremiah | Jeremiah 7–10 | August 2 |
| 216. "I Will Cause the Enemy to Entreat" | Jeremiah 11–15 | August 3 |
| 217. The Sin of Judah | Jeremiah 16–20 | August 4 |
| 218. Nebuchadnezzar, King of Babylon | Jeremiah 21–25 | August 5 |

| | | |
|---|---|---|
| 250. "Will Restore All That the Locust Ate" | Joel 1–3 | September 6 |
| 251. Fast, Pray, and Rest | -------------------- | September 7 |
| 252. "God's Judgment Was Coming" | Amos 1–2 | September 8 |
| 253. Against the Whole Family | Amos 3–5 | September 9 |
| 254. Woe to Them That Are at Ease in Zion | Amos 6–7 | September 10 |
| 255. Horror and Hope | Amos 8–9 | September 11 |
| 256. Mount Zion and Deliverance | Obadiah 1:1–21 | September 12 |
| 257. The Run-Away Prophet | Jonah 1–4 | September 13 |
| 258. Fast, Pray, and Rest | -------------------- | September 14 |
| 259. The Prophet Micah | Micah 1–2 | September 15 |
| 260. The Heads of Jacob, Princes | Micah 3–5 | September 16 |
| 261. Rejoice Not against My Enemy | Micah 6–7 | September 17 |
| 262. Nineveh Will Be Overthrown | Nahum 1–3 | September 18 |
| 263. Babylonia, the Chastening Rod | Habakkuk 1–3 | September 19 |
| 264. "Judgment Day Is Coming" | Zephaniah 1–3 | September 20 |
| 265. Fast, Pray, and Rest | -------------------- | September 21 |
| 266. The Unfinished Temple | Haggai 1–2 | September 22 |
| 267. The Temple Must Be Completed | Zechariah 1–2 | September 23 |
| 268. "The Lord Rebuke Thee, O Satan" | Zechariah 3–4 | September 24 |
| 269. "BRANCH" Will Build the Temple | Zechariah 5–6 | September 25 |
| 270. "Jealous of Zion" | Zechariah 7–8 | September 26 |
| 271. "Open Thy Doors, O Lebanon" | Zechariah 9–11 | September 27 |
| 272. Fast, Pray, and Rest | -------------------- | September 28 |
| 273. A Fountain Open to David's House | Zechariah 12–14 | September 29 |
| 274. "Will a Man Rob God?" | Malachi 1–4 | September 30 |
| 275. Jesus Christ, the Son of David | Matthew 1–4 | October 1 |
| 276. "The Beatitude" | Matthew 5–7 | October 2 |
| 277. Jesus Cleaned the Leper | Matthew 8–11 | October 3 |
| 278. Jesus Plucked Corn on the Sabbath | Matthew 12–15 | October 4 |
| 279. The Sadducees and Pharisees Tempted Jesus | Matthew 16–19 | October 5 |
| 280. "The Kingdom of Heaven" | Matthew 20–23 | October 6 |

| | | |
|---|---|---|
| 312. Fast, Pray, and Rest | -------------------- | November 7 |
| 313. The Beginning of Paul's Third Journey | Acts 19–20 | November 8 |
| 314. "Saul, Saul, Why Persecutest Thou Me?" | Acts 21–23 | November 9 |
| 315. "But Rise and Stand upon Thy Feet" | Acts 24–26 | November 10 |
| 316. Paul on His Journey to Rome | Acts 27–28 | November 11 |
| 317. "Vengeance Is Mine," Saith the Lord | Romans 1–3 | November 12 |
| 318. The Righteousness of God | Romans 4–5 | November 13 |
| 319. Fast, Pray, and Rest | -------------------- | November 14 |
| 320. "All Things Work Together for Good" | Romans 6–8 | November 15 |
| 321. "Pray to God for Israel, Brethren" | Romans 9–11 | November 16 |
| 322. "Present Your Body a Living Sacrifice" | Romans 12–16 | November 17 |
| 323. Paul Called to Be an Apostle of Christ | 1 Corinthians 1–6 | November 18 |
| 324. For the Earth Is the Lord's and the Fullness | 1 Corinthians 7–10 | November 19 |
| 325. "Take, Eat, This Is My Body" | 1 Corinthians 11–14 | November 20 |
| 326. Fast, Pray, and Rest | -------------------- | November 21 |
| 327. I Declare unto You the Gospel, Brethren | 1 Corinthians 15–16 | November 22 |
| 328. Paul and Timothy | 2 Corinthians 1–5 | November 23 |
| 329. Paul Sent Titus to Corinth | 2 Corinthians 6–9 | November 24 |
| 330. The Minority Accused Paul | 2 Corinthians 10–13 | November 25 |
| 331. Paul's Letter to the Galatians | Galatians 1–6 | November 26 |
| 332. The Christian's Heavenly "Bank Account" | Ephesians 1–6 | November 27 |
| 333. Fast, Pray, and Rest | -------------------- | November 28 |
| 334. Paul's Letter to the Philippians | Philippians 1–4 | November 29 |
| 335. The Head of the Body Is Christ | Colossians 1–4 | November 30 |
| 336. "A Holy Kiss" | 1 Thessalonians 1–5 | December 1 |
| 337. False Teaching | 2 Thessalonians 1–3 | December 2 |
| 338. Timothy, My Own Son in the Faith | 1 Timothy 1–3 | December 3 |
| 339. "The Love of Money, the Root of All Evil" | 1 Timothy 4–6 | December 4 |
| 340. "I Have Fought a Good Fight" | 2 Timothy 1–4 | December 5 |
| 341. The Young Pastor, Titus | Titus 1–3 | December 6 |
| 342. Fast, Pray, and Rest | -------------------- | December 7 |

# 4

# Appendix A

## (Personal Study Notes–Example)

Text:

_____

_____

Memory verse from text

_____

_____

_____

Reflection on text

_____

_____

_____

Action taken

_____

_____

_____

Testimony on acting on His Word

_____

_____

_____

# 5 Appendix B

**MY PRAYER REQUEST**— After reviewing and reflecting upon the specific text, go to God in prayer so that your request will be answered by Him.

_____

_____

_____

_____

_____

_____

_____

_____

_____

_____

_____

_____

_____

_____

_____

_____

# 6

# Appendix C

(A Few Important Bible References of
the Old and New Testaments)

## 10 COMMANDMENTS

THOU SHALT HAVE NO OTHER GODS BEFORE ME

THOU SHALT NOT MAKE UNTO THEE ANY GRAVEN IMAGE

THOU SHALT NOT TAKE THE NAME OF THE LORD THY GOD IN VAIN

REMEMBER THE SABBATH DAY, TO KEEP IT HOLY

HONOR THY FATHER AND THY MOTHER

THOU SHALT NOT KILL

THOU SHALT NOT COMMIT ADULTERY

THOU SHALT NOT STEAL

THOU SHALT NOT BEAR FALSE WITNESS AGAINST THY NEIGHBOR

THOU SHALT NOT COVET

TEMPTATION


JESUS WAS TEMPTED  BY THE DEVIL AFTER
FASTING FOR 40 DAYS AND 40 NIGHTS


MATTHEW 4:1-11

THE ORIGINAL 12 APOSTLES

SIMON PETER

JAMES

JOHN

ANDREW

PHILIP

THOMAS

NATHANIEL

MATTHEW

JAMES (THE LESSER)

SIMON (THE ZEALOT)

THADDEUS

JUDAS ISCARIOT

## THE 12 TRIBES OF ISRAEL

REUBEN

SIMEON

LEVI

JUDAH

DAN

NAPHTALI

GAD

ASHER

ISSACHAR

ZEBULUN

JOSEPH

BENJAMIN

THE PRAYER OF JABEZ

JABEZ CALLED TO THE GOD OF ISRAEL, AND GOD GRANTED HIS REQUEST; "OH, YOU WILL BLESS ME, AND ENLARGE MY TERRITORY; LET YOU HAND BE WITH ME, AND KEEP ME FROM HARM, SO THAT I WILL BE FREE FROM PAIN."

1 CHRONICLES 4:10

BIBLE REFERENCES:

1 Chronicles 16:8

Genesis 12:8

Job 12:4

Psalm 55:16

Psalm 116:2-4

Jeremiah 33:3-5

## THE 23<sup>RD</sup> PSALM

## PSALM 23

The Lord is my shepherd; I shall not want.

He maketh me to lie down in green pastures; he leadeth me beside the still waters.

He restoreth my soul; he leadeth me in the paths of righteousness for his name's sake

Yea, though I walk through the valley of the shadow of death, I will fear no evil; for thou art with me; thy rod and thy staff they comfort me.

Thou preparest a table before me in the presence of mine enemies; thou anointest my head with oil.; my cup runneth over.

Surely goodness and mercy shall follow me all the days of my life.; and I will dwell in the house of the Lord forever.

## THE BEATITUDES

- Blessed are the poor in spirit, for theirs is the kingdom of heaven.

- Blessed are they who mourn, for they shall be comforted

- Blessed are the meek, for they shall inherit the earth.

- Blessed are they who hunger and thirst for righteousness, for they shall be satisfied

- Blessed are the merciful, for they shall obtain mercy

- Blessed are the pure of heart, for they shall see God.

- Blessed are the peacemakers, for they shall be called children of God

- Blessed are they who are persecuted for the sake of righteousness, for theirs is the kingdom of heaven

## THE LAST SUPPER

Father, forgive them, for they know not what they do."
Luke. 23: 34 kjv

"This day thou shalt be with me in Paradise."
Luke. 23: 43 dra

Woman, behold thy son."
Jn. 19: 26-7 kjv

"My God, My God, why hast thou forsaken me?"
Matthew 27:46 kjv

«I thirst.»
John 19:28 kjv

"It is finished."

Jn 19: 30 kjv

"Father, into thy hands I commend my spirit."
Luke  23:46 kjv

THE 10 PLAGUES OF EGYPT


WATER TO BLOOD – EXODUS 7:14-23

FROGS – EXODUS 7:25

GNATS OR LICE – EXODUS 8:16-19

FLIES – EXODUS 8:20-32

LIVESTOCK DISEASE - EXODUS 9:1-7

BOILS - EXODUS: 9:8-12

THUNDER AND HAIL - EXODUS 9:13-35

LOCUSTS – EXODUS 10:1-20

DARKNESS – EXODUS 10:21-29

FIRST BORN – EXODUS 11: 1-12

# Gallery

# References

The Holy Bible, version and type including: King's James Version (KJV), DRA, NKJV, NIV

The Harris's Bible Commentary

# 8 About the Author

**ELDER CHARLES B. HARRIS Sr., BSc, civil engineering, is a retired engineer who has been chosen by God to transfer his engineering skills in promoting the work of the Lord. In the past, Elder Harris, who is a devoted Christian, had been accustomed to designing and constructing roads and houses. "For many are called, but few are chosen"** (Matthew 22:14). Elder Harris is one of those servants of God who was called to work for the Lord in writing *A Daily Journey Through The Year With God.* Elder Harris and his wife Victoria G. Harris have been married for 42 years, with four children and five grandchildren. He praises the Lord for His continued blessings upon him and his entire family.

Recall that God called Moses from the **burning bush** to lead his people out of bondage after being in Egypt for 430 years. **Moses was a builder, but he was also a great leader who loved the Lord** (Exodus 12:40–41).

There were other professionals that the good Lord also used in the past to carry out His work, and they are as follows: Jesus, a carpenter; Luke, a physician; Noah, a shipbuilder; Peter, James, John, and others, all who were fishermen. Matthew was a tax collector, Rev. Dr. Abayomi Noibi, an environmental engineer; Rev. Gbegbe Henry Fumbah, a computer engineer; Rev. Dr. William BGK Harris, an electrical engineer; Rev. Theophilus Massaquoi, a pilot; Pastor E. Shadrach Deline**,** a barber; and the list goes on. Therefore, Elder Harris hopes and prays that this *A Daily Journey Through The Year With God* will serve as an inspiration for winning souls to Christ.

To God be the glory for the knowledge, understanding, patience,
and wisdom given him to write this book.

Printed in the United States
by Baker & Taylor Publisher Services